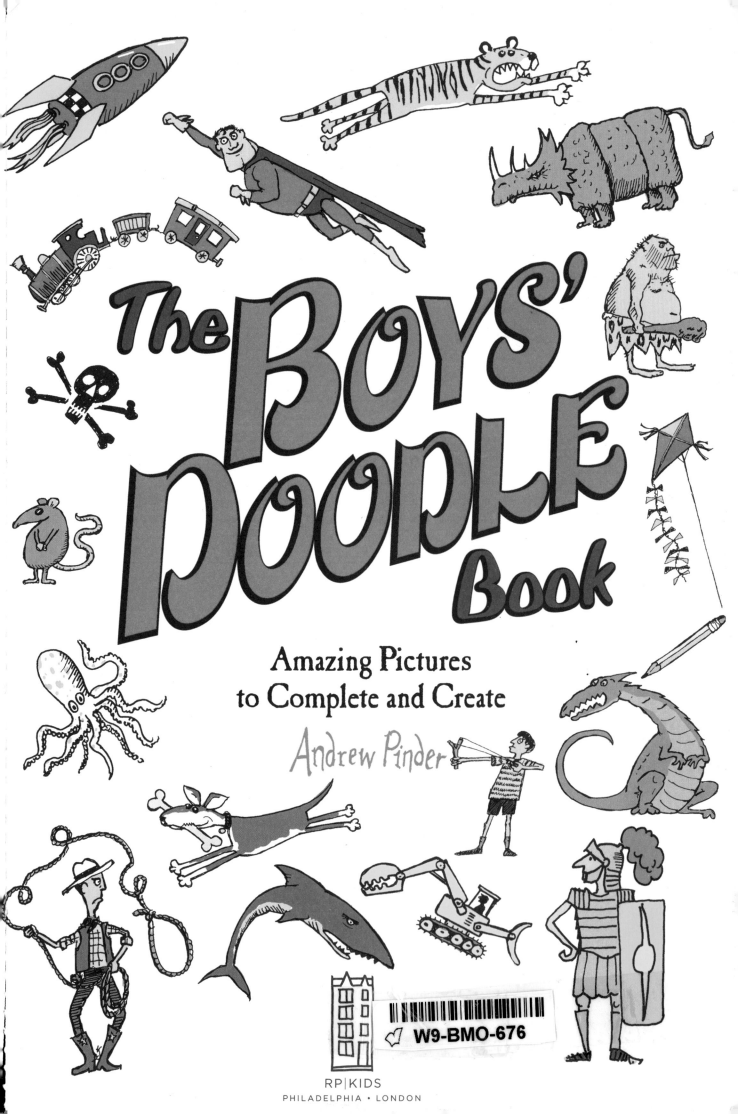

The Boys' Doodle Book

Amazing Pictures
to Complete and Create

Andrew Pinder

RP|KIDS
PHILADELPHIA · LONDON

Illustrated by Andrew Pinder

Copyright © 2013 by Buster Books

All rights reserved under the Pan-American and International Copyright Conventions

First published in Great Britain in 2008 by Buster Books,
an imprint of Michael O'Mara Books Limited, 9 Lion Yard, Tremadoc Road, London SW4 7NQ.

First published in the United States by Running Press Book Publishers, 2008

Printed in China

Books published by Running Press are available at special discounts for bulk purchases in the United States
by corporations, institutions, and other organizations. For more information, please contact the
Special Markets Department at the Perseus Books Group, 2300 Chestnut Street, Suite 200, Philadelphia,
PA 19103, or call (800) 810-4145, ext. 5000, or e-mail special.markets@perseusbooks.com.

ISBN 978-0-7624-5291-0

12 11 10 9 8
Digit on the right indicates the number of this printing

This edition published by:
Running Press Kids
An Imprint of Running Press Book Publishers
A Member of the Perseus Books Group
2300 Chestnut Street
Philadelphia, PA 19103–4371

Visit us on the web!
www.runningpress.com/kids

Invent a robot.

Alien invasion!

If only I had feet!

Make their shields scary.

Add Wild Bill's bucking bronco.

Whoops!

Help! Get me out of here.

Shiver m'timbers—what's in the chest?

Ooh, shiny!

Who is your hero?

For Your
Eyes Only

Spaceship
New Design

$$E = mc^2$$

$$A + x \sqrt{\frac{z^2 \ln + z}{\ln \theta}}$$

$$\frac{2\pi}{R} \sqrt[q]{\frac{2v}{\ln} * \frac{2v^2 + z}{\ln}} = \frac{2v}{\ln} \sqrt[q]{A + z} \sqrt{mz} = 3.20 ?$$

What animal is nibbling his toes?

Finish the castle.

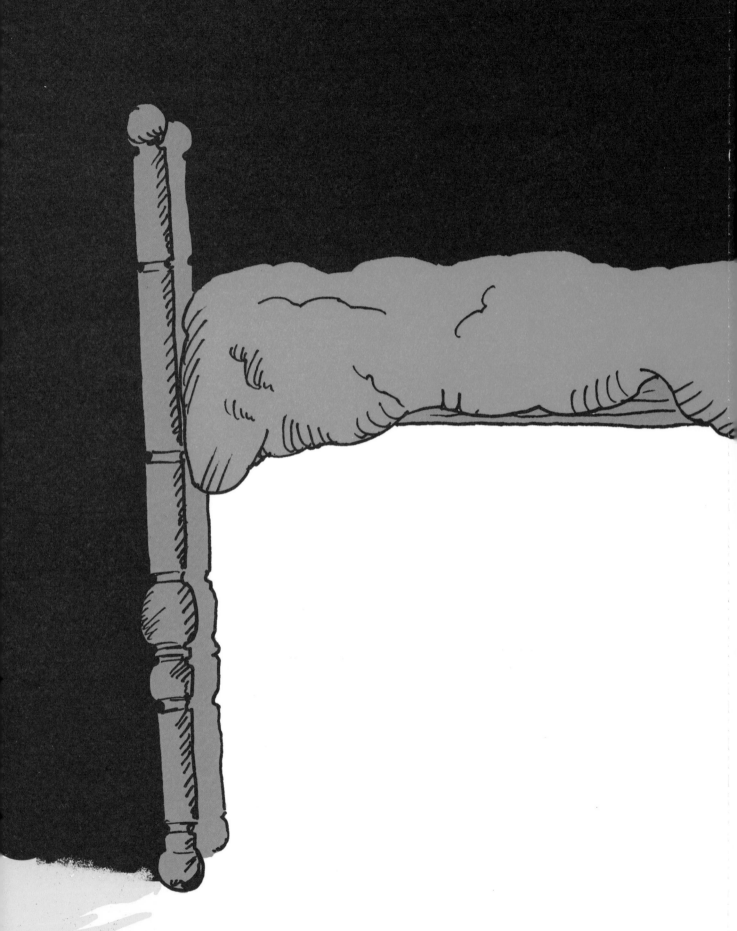

What's under the bed?

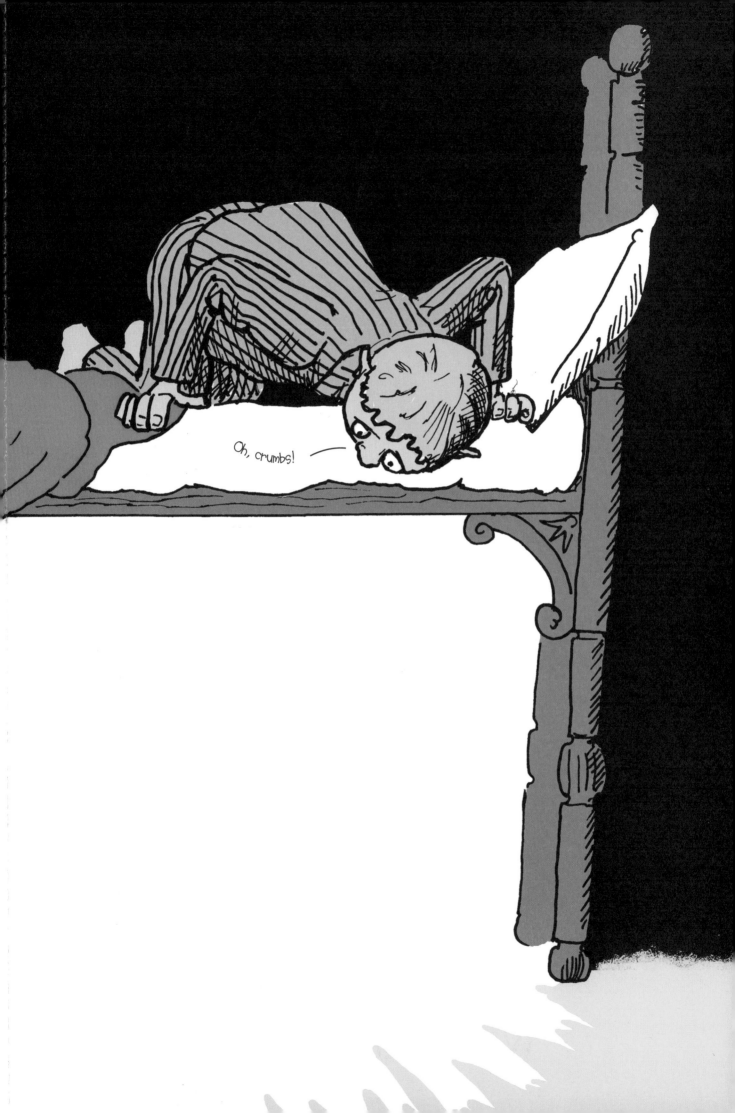

WANTED
DEAD OR ALIVE

ONE-EYED JAKE

$1000
REWARD

Draw Dr. Frankenstein's monster.

At last, Herr Doctor, it lives!

What's down there?

Design their superhero costumes.

What spooked him?

What's he laughing at?

What are the lions hunting?

Retreat!

What is hunting the lions?

What did he lasso?

Ship ahoy!

Sketch in some slimy specimens.

Build them a space city . . .

...and their dogs a space kennel.

Yuck!

Who is hunting for presents?

Finish the toboggan run.

What is his excuse?

He shoots . . . he scores!

Who is watching Coco the Clown?

Abracadabra!

Draw a dreadful dragon.

What did he do?

What hatched from the dino eggs?

Draw him some armor.

Design an incredible flying machine.

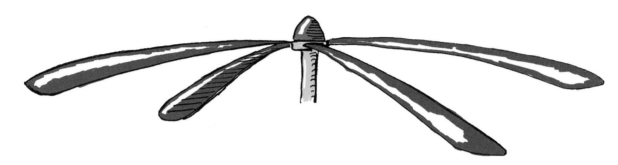

— But will it fly?

Surf's up!

What's in the cave?

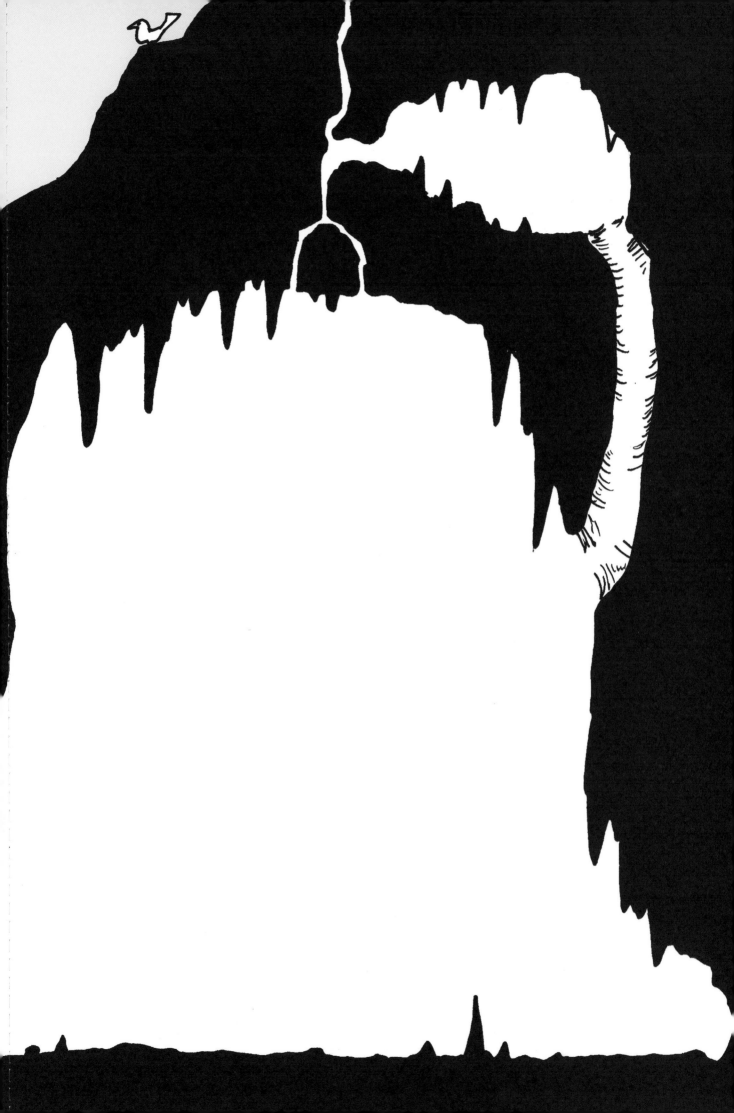

Finish the treasure map.

Make his hair look cool.

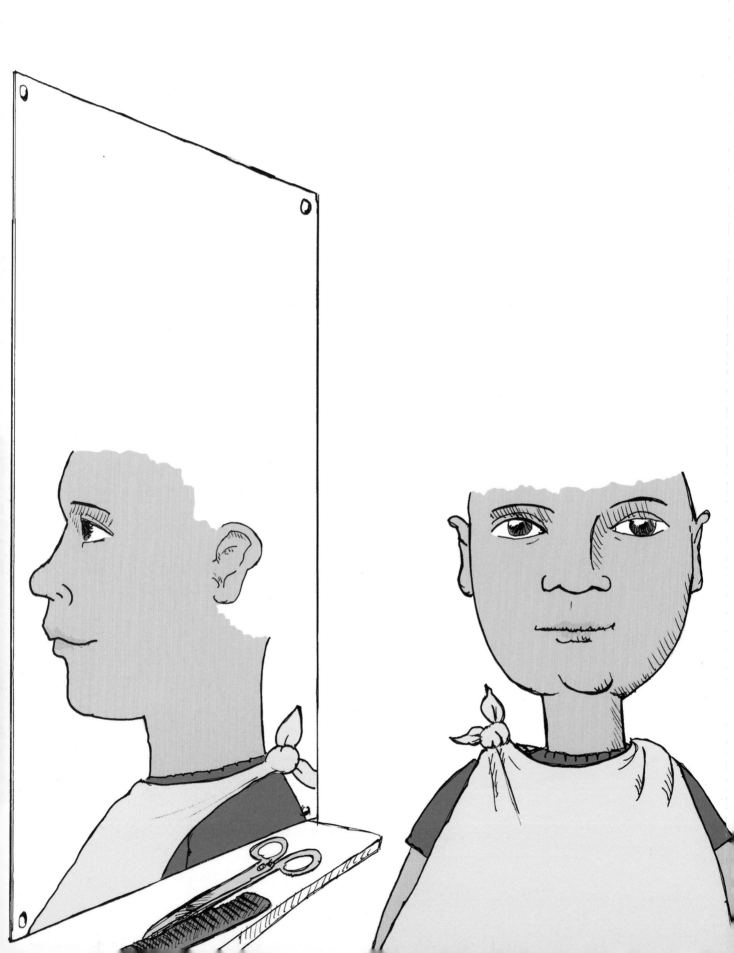

Sweet dreams . . .

Who is sitting on the eggs?

What's happening in the castle?

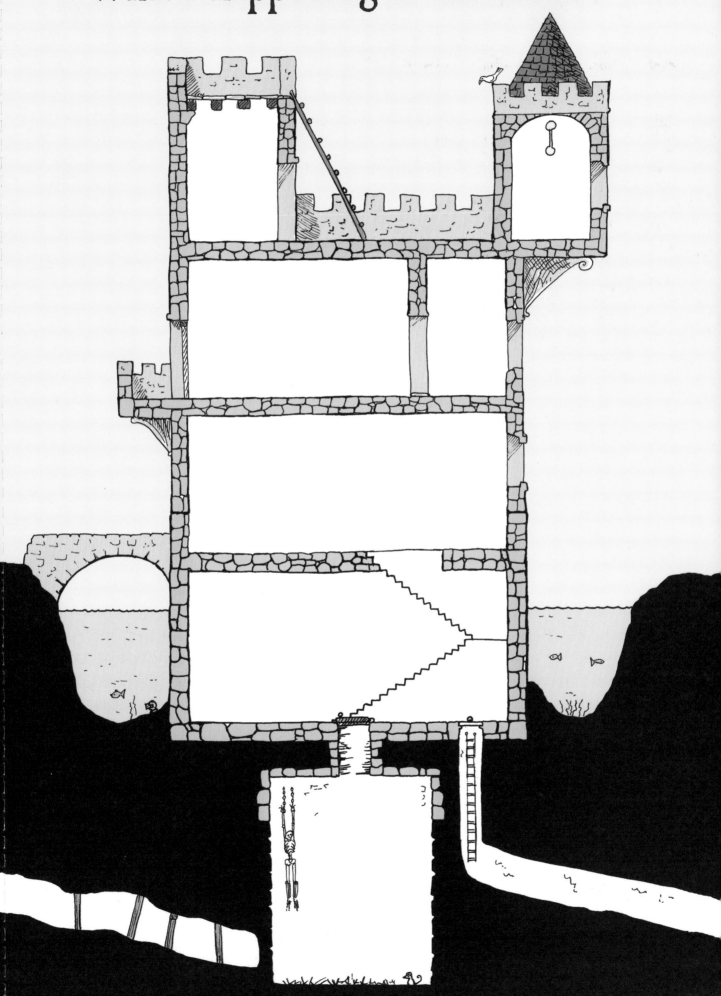

Complete the circus trick.

Launch the rocket.

10, 9, 8, 7, 6, 5, 4, 3, 2, 1 . . . Lift off!

Complete the monster.

TAP, TAP, TAP...

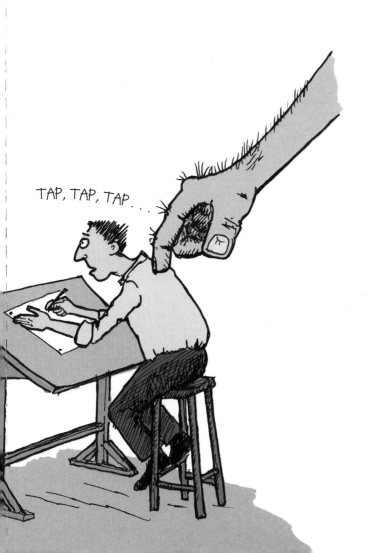

What did these ants build?

Very pleas-ant.

Construct a cool tree house.

Who is visiting the haunted house?

Fix the bridge and save the people.

What is he jumping over?

What is twisting in the tornado?

Design a great gadget.

What went bang in the night?

Draw their dinner . . .

But I'm a vegetarian.

. . . and their dessert.

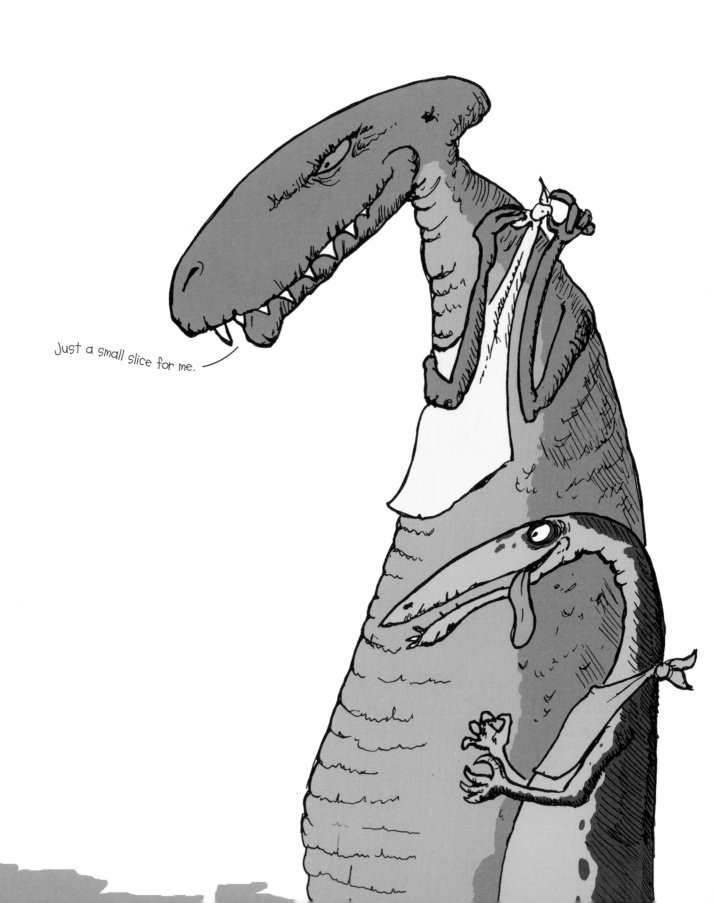

What a weird alien.

Draw his planet.

Oh no! A supervillain.

Who will save us?

What are his evil powers?

Bring a superhero to the rescue.

Save us superone . . .

What are his superpowers?

Who is crossing the river . . .

. . . and how?

What scared him?

Run!

What is he lifting?

Where are they visiting?

Design a monster truck.

Cool!

Captain Jack.

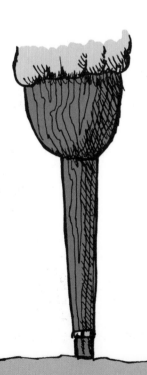

What is eating the bait?

Why is the caveman fleeing?

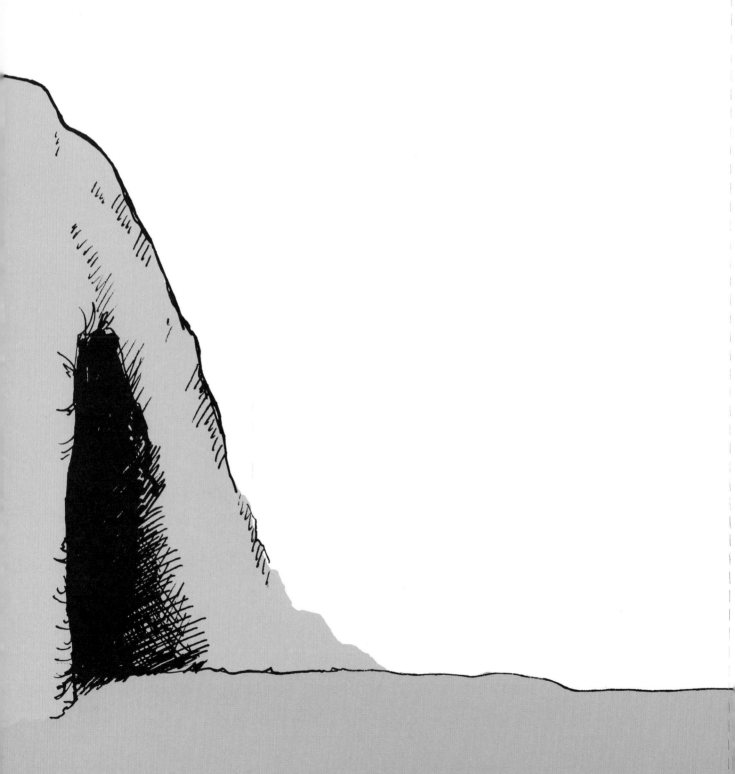

Finish the balls.

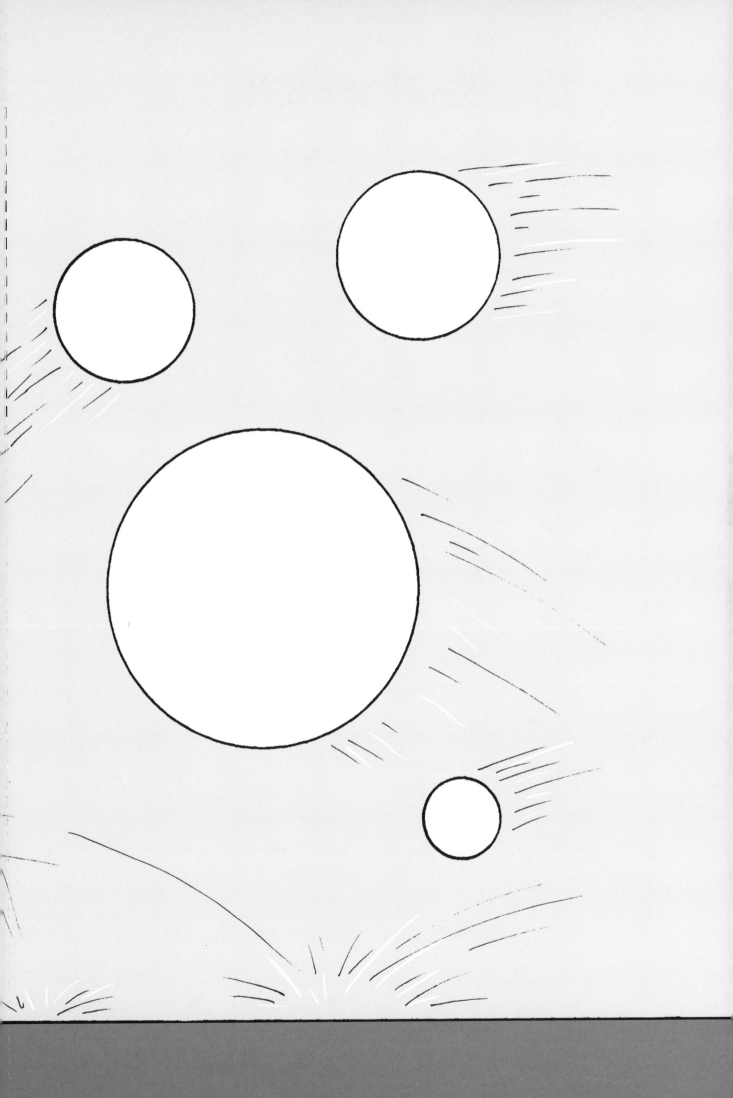

Complete the Viking fleet.

What's cooking?

Draw the firefighters . . .

. . . putting out the fire.

Stop the thief.

What is happening in the big top?

What's in the haunted mine?

Can you stop the stampede?

— Darn it.

Disguise the spy.

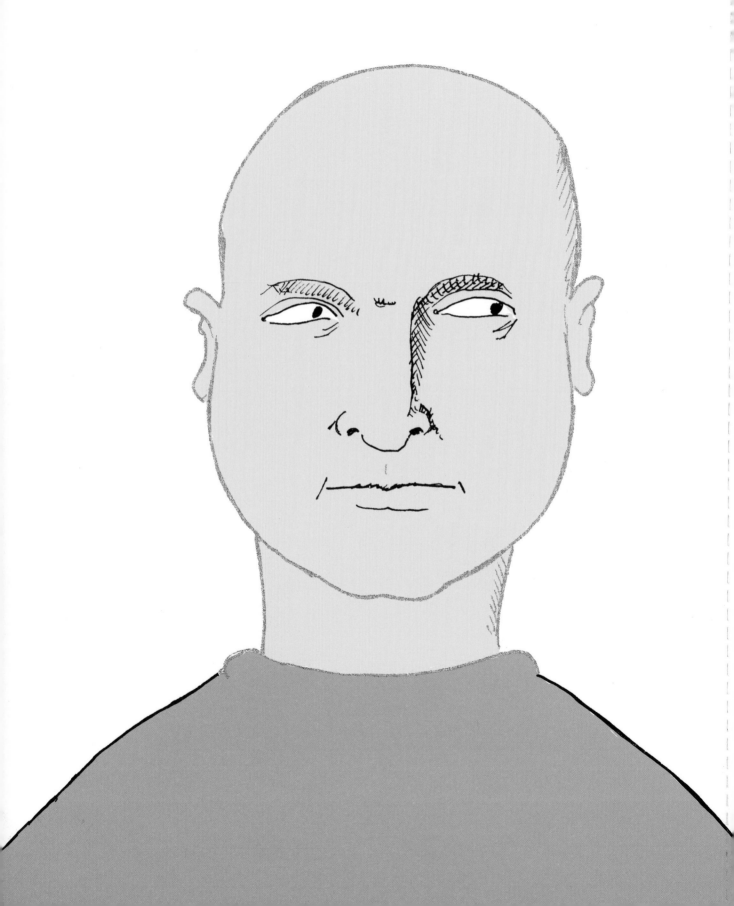

Make a yummy pizza for yourself . . .

. . . and a disgusting one for someone else.

What's in the pyramid?

Design the scariest roller coaster ever.

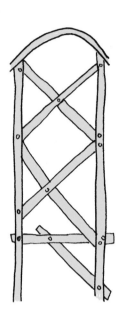

EXIT
NO REFUNDS

Save yourselves!

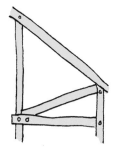

Who is bouncing?

Where are they going to land?

Not quite where I planned.

Invent a huge ice cream.

Why is he going bananas?

Who is next in the mud bath?

Draw what he turned into.

Ghosts!

At least they aren't screaming
at us for a change.

Finish my skeleton, please.

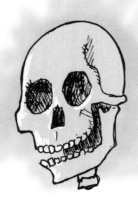

And mine!

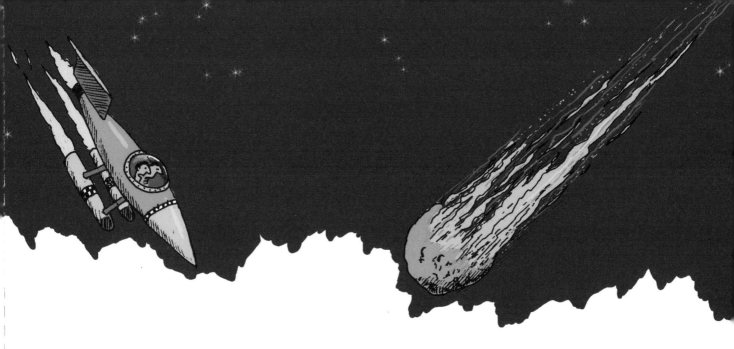

Help them save planet Earth.

Draw him a flying machine.

What's so funny?

What is he aiming at?

Finish the domino cascade.

What will they find
on the forbidden
planet?

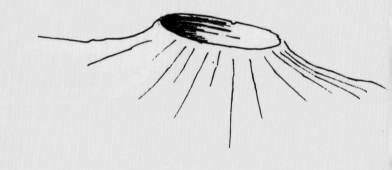

Don't look down!

Complete their cave complex.

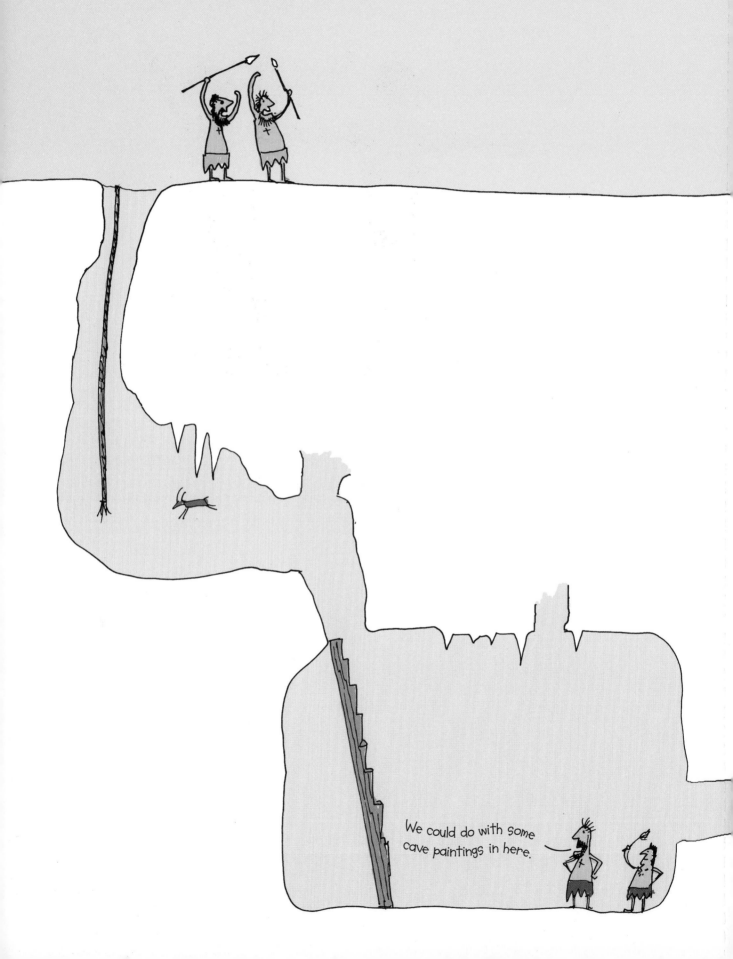

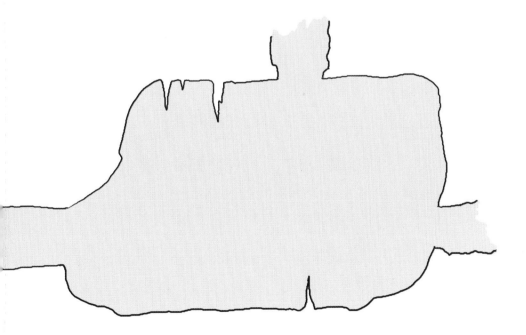

Spotty . . . or stripey?

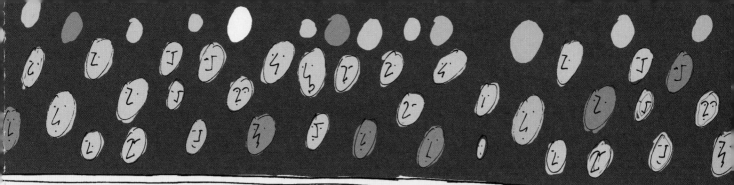

Who is the gladiator too
scared to fight?

Decorate the Greek temple.

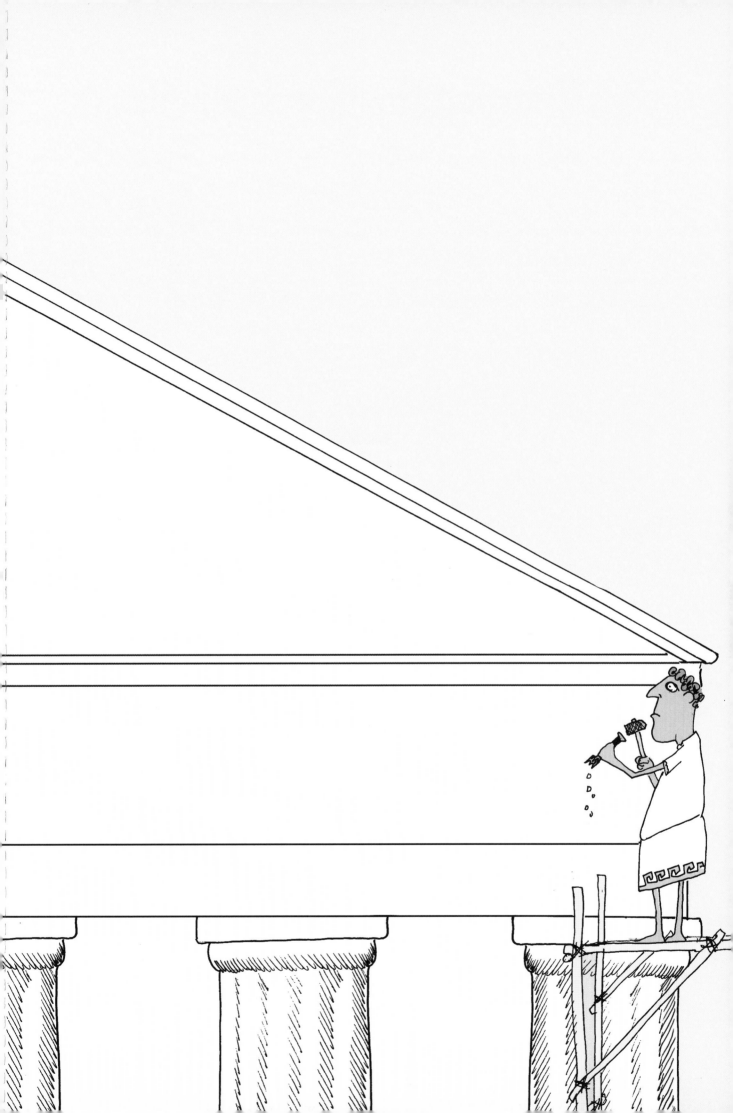

Make his cycling gear really bright.

Give them clown faces.

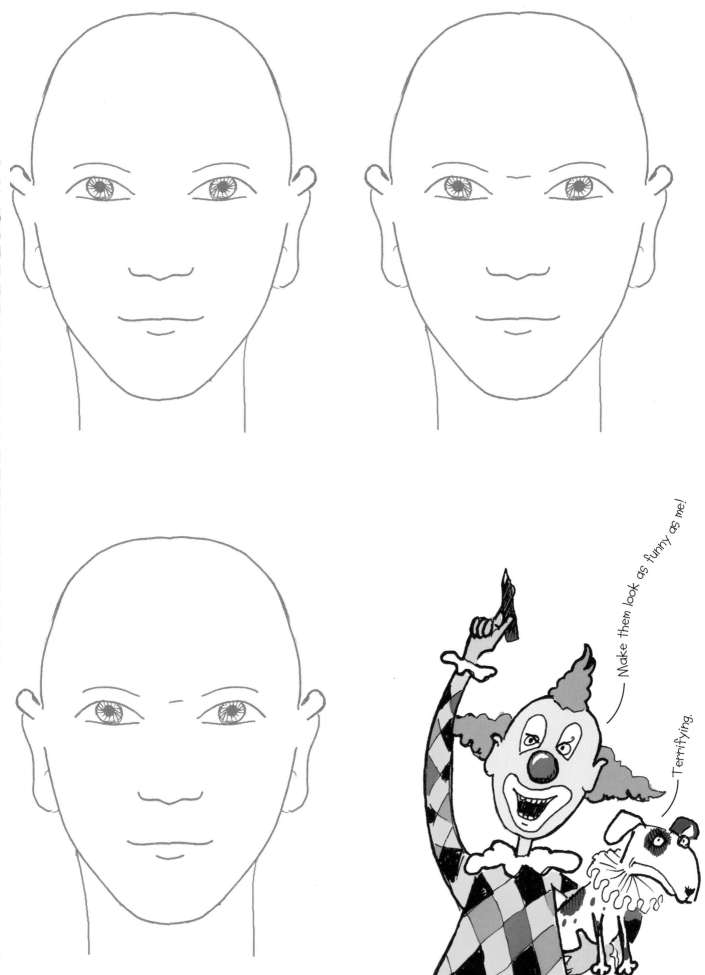

Make them look as funny as me!

Terrifying.

Build him a device to get the coconuts down.

What is on his X-ray?

What has the hippopotamus eaten?

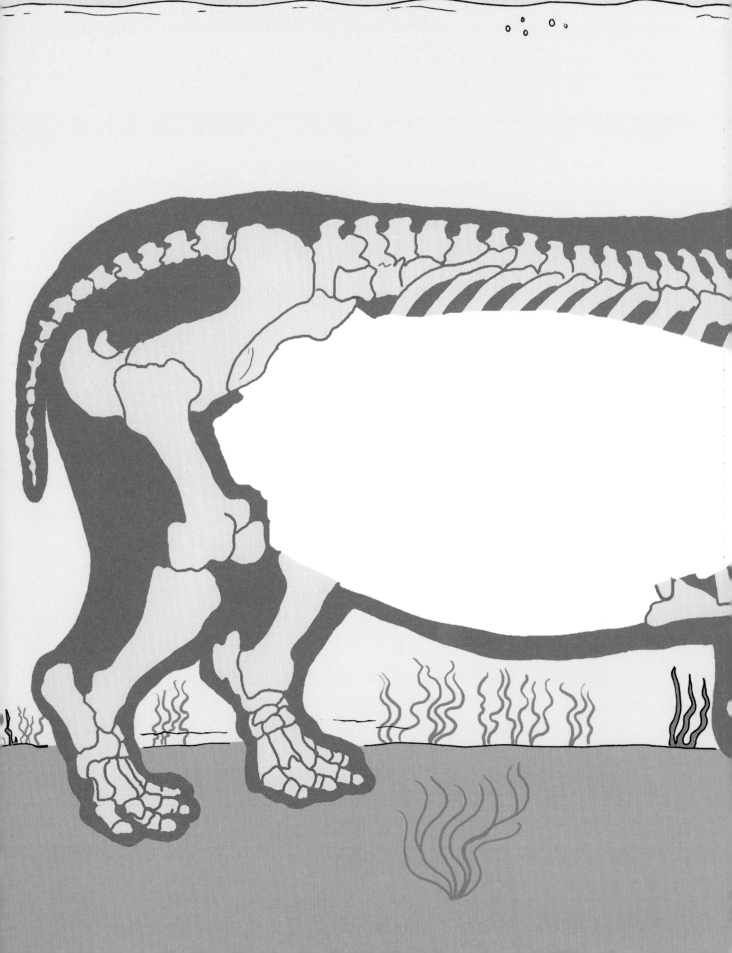

If you could go anywhere, where would you go?

Who's coming down
the beanstalk?

Create a machine to knock down the castle.

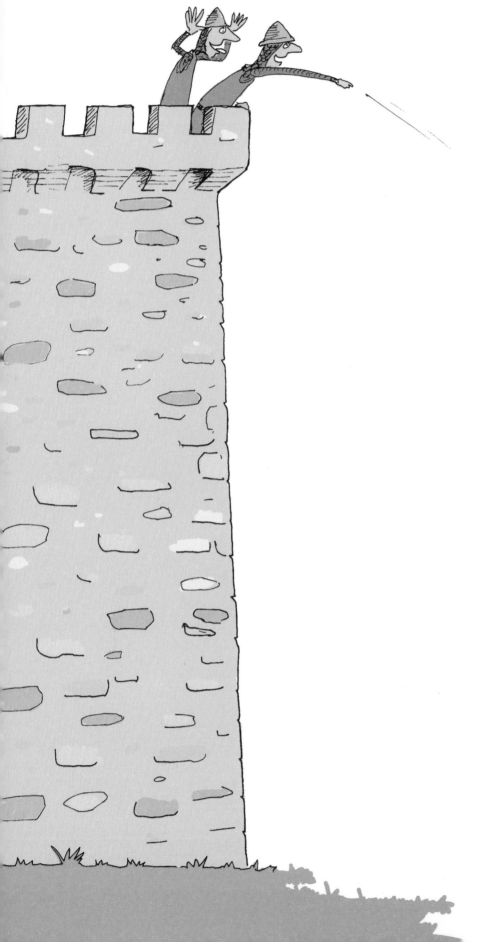

Design a supercool computer game.

What gadgets are in the latest spy kit?

Send a lifeboat and a rescue helicopter.